She Persisted

SALLY RIDE

—INSPIRED BY—

She Persisted

by Chelsea Clinton & Alexandra Boiger

SALLY RIDE

Written by
Atia Abawi

Interior illustrations by
Gillian Flint

PHILOMEL

PHILOMEL BOOKS
An imprint of Penguin Random House LLC, New York

First published in the United States of America by Philomel,
an imprint of Penguin Random House LLC, 2021.

Text copyright © 2021 by Chelsea Clinton.
Illustrations copyright © 2021 by Alexandra Boiger.

Visit us online at penguinrandomhouse.com.

LIBRARY OF CONGRESS CATALOGING-IN-PUBLICATION DATA:
Names: Abawi, Atia, author. | Flint, Gillian, illustrator. Title: Sally Ride / written
by Atia Abawi ; interior illustrations by Gillian Flint. Description: New York :
Philomel Books, 2021. | Series: She persisted | Includes bibliographical references. |
Audience: Ages 6–9 | Audience: Grades 2–3 | Summary: "A biography of Sally Ride
in the She Persisted series"— Provided by publisher. Identifiers: LCCN 2020047610
| ISBN 9780593115923 (hardcover) | ISBN 9780593115930 (trade paperback) | ISBN
9780593115947 (ebook) Subjects: LCSH: Ride, Sally—Juvenile literature. | United
States. National Aeronautics and Space Administration—Biography—Juvenile
literature. | Women astronauts—United States—Biography—Juvenile literature. |
Astronauts—United States—Biography—Juvenile literature. | Women physicists—
United States—Biography—Juvenile literature. Classification: LCC TL789.85.R53
A235 2021 | DDC 629.450092 [B]—dc23
LC record available at https://lccn.loc.gov/2020047610

Printed in the United States of America

HC ISBN 9780593115923
PB ISBN 9780593115930

10 9 8 7 6 5 4 3 2 1

Edited by Jill Santopolo.
Design by Ellice M. Lee.
Text set in LTC Kennerley.

For
my daughter, Elin, and my son, Arian:
there are no limits to your dreams
as long as you keep persisting.

She
Persisted

....

Dear Reader,

As Sally Ride and Marian Wright Edelman both powerfully said, "You can't be what you can't see." When Sally Ride said that, she meant that it was hard to dream of being an astronaut, like she was, or a doctor or an athlete or anything at all if you didn't see someone like you who already had lived that dream. She especially was talking about seeing women in jobs that historically were held by men.

I wrote the first *She Persisted* and the books that came after it because I wanted young girls—and children of all genders—to see women who worked hard to live their dreams. And I wanted all of us to see examples of persistence in the face of different challenges to help inspire us in our own lives.

I'm so thrilled now to partner with a sisterhood of writers to bring longer, more in-depth versions of these stories of women's persistence and achievement to readers. I hope you enjoy these chapter books as much as I do and find them inspiring and empowering.

And remember: If anyone ever tells you no, if anyone ever says your voice isn't important or your dreams are too big, remember these women. They persisted and so should you.

Warmly,
Chelsea Clinton

SALLY
RIDE

TABLE OF CONTENTS

. . . .

. . . .

California Girl

S ally Kristen Ride was born a California girl. She loved the taste of the sun on her face and wind in her hair. She was smart and sassy. She was energetic and strong. She was a diehard Los Angeles Dodgers fan, dreaming of one day playing shortstop for them. Sally did not grow up wanting to be an astronaut, but life would lead her down a path of hard work, luck and privilege that would eventually make her the first American woman in space.

Sally Ride was born on May 26, 1951, on a sunny yet cool Saturday in Southern California. Her parents, Dale and Joyce Ride, said she was an active toddler who knew what she wanted and would stop at nothing to get it. This was a trait that would follow her throughout her life. Her first word was "no," giving little Sally a powerful tool to let those around her understand what she wanted—and didn't want—before she could even form full sentences. Letting the people around her know what she wanted was something Sally did her whole life. And since her little toddler tongue had trouble pronouncing *Sally*, she referred to herself as "Sassy," a nickname that fit her personality. She was two years old when her younger sister Karen was born. But because little "Sassy" couldn't pronounce her sister's name, she ended up calling her "Pear," which led to "Bear"—a name that would stick through adulthood.

Although there was not a lot of hugging, kissing or whispered *I love yous* in the Ride household while Sally was growing up, there was stability, encouragement and tons of love. Dale and Joyce were open-minded people who raised their daughters without worrying about what people said girls or boys should do in that time. In the 1950s and the 1960s, most girls were taught that they weren't as strong, smart or tough as boys. But Sally's parents wanted their daughters to believe they could do anything boys could do, and they encouraged their girls in everything that they tried. Not everyone felt this way back then; many felt boys and girls should do different things from each other and that they had their designated roles.

"We wanted our daughters to excel, not conform," Joyce once explained.

Dale said that he always encouraged his daughters to go after their passions, and always allowed them to explore.

"There was absolutely no sense—through all the years growing up—that there was any limit to what I could do or what I could pursue," Sally later said.

When Sally was nine years old, that sense of exploration led the family to spend an entire year traveling throughout Europe. Her parents, with permission of the girls' school principal, took the children out of school in 1961 and drove a station wagon from one European country to another and from city to city. The girls learned about different cultures, saw new sites and met new and

interesting people—all of which opened Sally's and Bear's eyes to a big, beautiful world outside of America. Sally rode in the front passenger seat as the family navigator with a map in her hand (back then people didn't know of the dangers of children sitting in the front like they do today). Her father was at the wheel, and her mom and sister rode in the back providing the family with jingly tunes to pass the time.

It was in Spain that Joyce taught Sally how to play tennis, a sport she would grow to love and excel at. Sally was an exceptionally talented athlete. She loved baseball, football, really any kind of sport with a ball and even those without! Sally would play with the neighborhood kids back home in California and wasn't afraid of getting dirty. But she hated being called a tomboy!

"*Tomboy*, when applied to a girl, means a girl acting like a boy. As opposed to a girl acting like a girl," Sally told a reporter when she was older.

Despite her rough-and-tumble nature, young

Sally was also shy. She didn't like to be called on in class even if she knew the answer to the teacher's question. She would huddle down in her chair hoping the teacher wouldn't notice her. Sally was an introvert, which meant she didn't like too much attention and enjoyed spending time with herself or those she felt closest to.

But Sally was born to shine, which sometimes conflicted with that introverted nature.

CHAPTER 2

Science and Sports

S ally was naturally smart and athletic. Her blue eyes sparkled with determination, fascination and charm throughout her life.

On top of that, from a very young age Sally was fascinated by science. To help foster her interest, her parents got her a chemistry set as well as a subscription to *Scientific American* magazine when she was in elementary school—which she would read from cover to cover. They also bought her a telescope. Through that lens, Sally would marvel at the complexities of the moon, planets and stars. Orion was her favorite constellation.

Sally loved to learn new things when inspiration struck, but she wasn't always the best student—despite being so smart and skipping fifth grade for high test scores. Oftentimes she would put off her homework or studying for tests until the car ride to school. The best teachers knew how to motivate Sally's curiosity and open her mind to new things. Some teachers, on the other hand, would get eye rolls and see her obvious disinterest. Just like when she was a toddler, she let it be known what worked for her and what didn't.

Sally's weekdays were spent at school and doing homework, but her weekends were all about tennis tournaments. She was quick on her feet, and her problem-solving mind helped her on the court as much as her athleticism. By the time she made it to eighth grade, Sally was ranked number twenty in Southern California for girls ages twelve and under. This achievement got her a partial tennis scholarship her sophomore year to the famed private high school Westlake School for Girls. This was the beginning of many doors opening for Sally, and many dreams coming true—some of which she didn't even know she had yet.

Through her high school years, Sally made

friends that would last a lifetime. Her hardworking, cheerful and dynamic personality was one that people wanted to be around. But Sally, still an introvert, preferred to keep her friends limited to those she felt most comfortable with.

As the years went on, Sally fell more and more in love with science. Back then, even more than now, many people said that science was just for boys. Luckily, Sally was surrounded by encouraging parents and teachers who knew otherwise. The only exception was one of her English teachers, who made her cry by stating that she was "too science-oriented" and "lacked creativity." The teacher said Sally had a mind that was wasted in science.

Sally persisted and focused on the teachers who inspired her, though, especially Dr. Elizabeth

Mommaerts, her human physiology teacher. Dr. Mommaerts was one of the few women to have earned a PhD in science at that time, and Sally was fascinated by her and her sharp brain. Sally would often bring her teacher intellectual puzzles and watch in amazement as Dr. Mommaerts solved them easily.

"She challenged me to be curious, ask questions and think for myself," Sally would later write. Sally saw Dr. Mommaerts as someone she wanted to model her own life after.

While she was a senior, Sally became the captain of her high school's tennis team and continued playing in tournaments throughout the country. The lessons Sally learned on the court, especially the ones about controlling her emotions and keeping a cool head, were ones that would help her

throughout life during intense situations. In particular, they were lessons that would come in handy when she joined NASA.

"Tennis taught me a lot about self-control," she said later. "Self-discipline. How to maintain a kind of relatively cool demeanor even when you're winning or losing by a lot."

In the spring of 1968, Sally graduated from Westlake and was on her way to college.

She decided to attend Swarthmore College in Pennsylvania, where she had received a full scholarship. This decision had her hop from the sunny West Coast to the cool and often chilly East Coast. At Swarthmore, Sally focused her studies on physics. Despite people saying it was for men, she knew it was what she wanted to continue learning about. She also played as the number one seed—or top player—for the school's tennis team, and joined the basketball and field hockey teams as well. But even with all of that keeping her busy, things just didn't feel right there for Sally. She was homesick.

And on top of that, Sally was thinking hard about her future. She decided to put her studies on the back burner to focus on tennis. Sally wanted to see whether she could make it as a professional tennis player.

"I had this very, very strong feeling that I had something in me that I hadn't really explored," she would later recall. Sally wondered whether she could pursue her tennis dream to its fullest extent, and whether she was good enough to make it to the professional circuit. She knew she could not wait to find out. "If I wait[ed] until after I graduate[d], it would likely be too late," she said later. And so, after thinking hard about this decision for several weeks, Sally called her parents and told them she wanted to come home.

································

Dreams Can Change

When Sally came back home, she threw herself into tennis, making sure to practice each and every day. This was her chance to see whether she was good enough to become a professional tennis player and champion.

But she didn't stop her studies entirely. She continued to take some classes at nearby UCLA while pursuing her tennis dream.

Her focus, though, was on training—every

day and some evenings under the glow of the moon and the sparkle of the stars that made up Orion.

But in life, dreams can often change, and they did for Sally. After months of prioritizing her tennis game, persisting and putting in all of the hours and hard work, Sally realized she just did not enjoy the tough regimental grit it took to be a professional athlete. It was difficult and draining, and not nearly as much fun for her as she thought following her dreams should be.

But the now-older "Sassy" knew what she wanted to do. While it was disappointing to give up on her tennis dream, Sally's focus shifted to another passion: science.

"I realized finally and for certain . . . that my education, science, was more important to me than tennis was," Sally would later recall.

But tennis helped Sally once more: She was accepted to Stanford University in Northern California by the same man who had once been the dean of admissions at Swarthmore. This time he was recruiting her to play tennis at Stanford while accepting her into what was then a mostly male physics department. So Sally packed up her red Toyota Corona and made the drive to start her latest adventure.

Many people at that time thought that physics wasn't a good subject for women to study. They thought women couldn't handle it. And some people at Stanford agreed. One male professor is said to have stood up and declared, "What are these girls doing here? You are taking jobs away from men!"

But Sally persisted because she knew what she wanted. She had been raised to believe she could do anything a man could do. And so she asserted herself with confidence and determination, focusing on her work and not the naysayers.

During her summers her former passion became her hobby. In 1972, while teaching tennis, Sally got to meet tennis legend Billie Jean King. King told Sally that if she continued to practice and work hard, she could make it to the pro tour. But Sally's heart belonged to science now.

She spent eight years at Stanford, receiving her undergraduate, her graduate and then her doctorate degrees—earning her title as a physicist.

Sally absolutely loved physics. She marveled at how it helped explain everything, from the formation of the cosmos and the rocky and green lands she lived on to the way a tennis ball flew and curved through the air after someone smacked it with their racket.

Sally hoped to transition from student to teacher. She enjoyed the classroom, and she loved learning and then sharing her knowledge with others to help them understand the beauty of science.

But in 1977, her life would change at the school cafeteria as she was munching on some scrambled eggs and a cinnamon roll. That's when she glanced through the school newspaper and read the headline: *NASA to recruit women.*

Almost a decade prior, in 1969, while she was

still at Swarthmore, Sally had watched the moon
landing in awe—along with the rest of the world.
But even as she hung posters of lunar photographs
on her wall, it had never crossed her mind that she
would get the chance to go to space. Most astronauts were military test pilots, and more glaringly,
they were all men.

"I just assumed there would never be a place for women," she said.

But here she was now, reading an article that would change her life and the course of American history. NASA was recruiting new astronauts, and for the first time, women could apply.

An unshakable excitement ran through Sally's body. She suddenly realized she had a new dream: she wanted to be an astronaut.

....

CHAPTER 4

Space Woman

With her new dream quickly taking hold, Sally knew she had to act. She had already learned that, in order to make dreams come true, you had to work hard and go after what you wanted. So she quickly wrote to NASA and requested an application to become a mission specialist in the space program.

NASA responded. But they also responded and sent applications out to 25,000 other hopefuls.

Out of those 25,000, a little more than 8,000 filled out the forms and sent them back to NASA—1,251 of them were women. As NASA continued to narrow down their applicants, they invited Sally to Houston, Texas, in August 1977, where the Johnson Space Center was located. There, Sally went through physical and mental examinations. Her athleticism impressed the doctors—she was tested on a treadmill and was able to jog super fast for seventeen straight minutes!

This trip also gave her the opportunity to confidently explain to her examiners why she wanted to be an astronaut. She wrote, "I think that my background (the scientific training in general, and astrophysics experience in particular) qualifies me to contribute as much to the program as I expect to get out of it." Astrophysics is the area of physics that focuses on stars and planets, and Sally studied it in graduate school.

Eventually NASA gave her the call she had been dreaming about.

"NASA chose me and my life took quite a turn," Sally said later.

And turn it did. She was one of thirty-five new astronauts chosen from the largest application pool in NASA's history! The new group of astronauts called themselves the Thirty-Five New Guys or TFNGs. Out of the thirty-five, six were white women (including Sally), three were African American men and one was an Asian American man.

Sally was excited but also nervous.

"I had no idea what to expect," she recalled. "I mean, what do you do when you're an astronaut?

Who knows? I don't even remember having specific goals, other than to fly in space!"

There were still many people who did not believe a woman could hack being an astronaut. Some of those people were within the walls of NASA itself—including some of the older astronauts. Legendary astronaut Chuck Yeager even sneered at one of the female astronauts and told her she was only along for the ride. But Sally kept her focus despite the criticism. She worked hard, she studied and she continued to exercise.

Sally and the five other woman astronauts felt

tremendous pressure to prove themselves. They wanted to show America, and the world, that they could do exactly what the men could do and what so many still believed they could not do. And more than anything else, they wanted to go to space. They persisted together.

The time would come when the bosses at NASA would select new space shuttle crews, including the first American woman to go to space. The Soviet Union, at the time America's great rival in many things, including the race to get to space, had already sent a woman, Valentina Tereshkova, to space in 1963. And they would send another, Svetlana Savitskaya, before the United States would send their first. America was losing the space race when it came to equality of the sexes.

NASA doesn't share how space shuttle crews are chosen. But for the decision makers, the focus fell on Sally. She was a scientist, an athlete, and someone who worked well under pressure. She also put more into her training at NASA than she ever had into tennis or anything else. Sally had finally found an unrelenting passion, and she fell in love with her new role as an astronaut. She wrote to her childhood friend Sue Okie, "I have lost my dominant trait, which has been not to work at things. I'm really working hard, and I'm enjoying it. In fact, I'm obsessed with it." She hadn't put much effort into classes that didn't motivate her at school, she hadn't felt like putting in the work necessary to become a tennis pro, but she would not give up on traveling to space—this passion burned strong and she would give it her all.

Sally's training involved intense studying, but it also included a lot of fun as the astronauts prepared for space flight. Among other things, they learned what the weightlessness of space would be like, and how to fly in jets, scuba dive, and use a parachute.

In April 1982, Sally received the news that NASA had chosen her to be the first American woman in space, though she would have to wait another year before that would happen.

During an interview before Sally's launch, reporter Lynn Sherr asked her if she thought she was as good as the male astronauts. Without hesitation, Sally answered, "Yeah."

On June 18, 1983, Sally woke before dawn and looked up at the sky, the way she had when she was a young girl in her backyard searching for her favorite constellation, Orion. This time she was doing it from Cape Canaveral, Florida, the morning of her first launch into space.

And then in *5 . . . 4 . . . 3 . . . 2 . . . 1 . . . liftoff!* Sally and her STS-7 mission team rumbled and rattled up through the sky and past Earth's atmosphere, safely making it into orbit on the space shuttle *Challenger*.

It was exhilarating to be in space, and Sally

wanted to savor the experience, but she knew she had a job to do, and one that she had to do right.

"I think there was quite a bit of extra pressure on me just to avoid mistakes," Sally later commented when talking about the stress of being the first American woman in space. She may have gone up as part of a crew of five, but all eyes were on her.

One of Sally's most important jobs during this flight was to operate a big robot arm she had helped design. The arm was made to deploy and grab satellites that were hurtling around Earth and store them in the *Challenger*'s cargo bay. She operated a joystick, almost like a video game, but this was not a game and it would be incredibly risky. If she missed grabbing the satellite, it could damage their ship—or pose dangers to other ships in the future. When the time came, though, after a few heart-pounding moments, Sally was able to breathe a sigh of relief: she had done it!

"I certainly felt proud," she said when reflecting upon that moment later on. "I think anyone would have under those circumstances. It made me all the more determined to do things right. And to look professional while I was up there."

And professional she was. She made sure to get all of the jobs assigned to her done. But Sally also took the time to appreciate where she was. She viewed Earth from an angle most humans never get to see outside of pictures.

The space shuttle raced around Earth every ninety minutes. Sally said that the sights she saw were unbelievable. "I could see coral reefs off the coast of Australia. A huge storm swirling in the ocean. I could see an enormous dust storm building over northern Africa," she explained.

Although she would zip herself up in her sleep restraint—kind of like a sleeping bag that would prevent her from floating around—she didn't sleep much while she was in space. Sally didn't want to miss anything! Sleep could wait for when she got home.

What really left an impact was the fragility of our home planet.

"I remember the first time that I looked towards the horizon," she recalled. "I saw the blackness of space, and then the bright blue Earth. And then I noticed right along the horizon it looked as if someone had taken a royal blue crayon and just traced along Earth's horizon. And then I realized that that blue line, that really thin royal blue line, was Earth's atmosphere, and that was all there was of it. And it's so clear from that perspective how fragile our existence is. It makes you appreciate how important it is to take care of that atmosphere."

It was an impression that would shape the rest of her life and life's work.

CHAPTER 5

After the Landing

ROGERS COMMISSION

After returning home safely, Sally continued her work with NASA. She ended up going to space again—this time with another woman astronaut, Kathryn Sullivan, who was her friend from the TFNGs. Sally was slotted to go a third time, but that trip was halted after the *Challenger* disaster. Seven astronauts from the STS-51-L mission team, including some of Sally's friends and a schoolteacher who was going to be the first civilian sent to space, lost their lives.

Sally was heartbroken by the loss of her friends. Making it hit even closer to home was the fact that the *Challenger* was the very same space shuttle that had taken her on her own previous space flights. So when President Ronald Reagan called for a government commission to investigate the accident and NASA asked Sally to be part of it, she knew it would be tough but very necessary. She wanted to know why her friends had died and to prevent any similar tragedies from happening in the future.

"I needed to know what the answer was and that NASA was going to do something to fix it," Sally said later.

Through their investigations in what became

known as the Rogers Commission, Sally was upset to find out that the explosion could have been prevented. The O-rings on the rockets malfunctioned, allowing hot gas to leak out when their job was to keep it in. That led to the fireball that tore the *Challenger* apart. One engineer had tried to warn his bosses before the launch that the O-rings would malfunction in cold temperatures, but no one listened to him. And the morning of the launch, the weather was frigid with near-freezing temperatures as the world watched the spacecraft blow up in the sky. Sally helped expose the truth despite it pointing the finger of fault at some of the very people who had helped make her the first American woman in space.

After this tragic failure, NASA decided to stop their missions into space for a while so they could work out safety issues. Sally took this as her cue to start thinking about life after NASA.

THE RIDE REPORT

But before leaving the space program, Sally had one more job, and that was to help figure out the future of NASA. She spent a year in Washington, D.C., compiling what eventually became known as *The Ride Report* (the official title was *Leadership and America's Future in Space*).

The Ride Report consisted of four main initiatives to restore America's leadership when it came to the space program.

1—Send humans to Mars.

Sally believed that settling Mars should be a goal, and that NASA should set up a Martian base. But because it takes about a year, or possibly even up to two years, to get to Mars and back, this would need to be carefully planned. No more space races, she recommended. Competition and races made the explorations more dangerous and less accurate.

2—Build an outpost on the moon.

Sally hoped NASA could one day also construct a lunar outpost on the moon to better explore its resources.

3—Explore the solar system robotically.

Although not as exciting as human exploration, Sally believed that robots could give us even better opportunities to research other planets and celestial bodies, such as comets and asteroids, at least at first.

4—Launch a mission to Planet Earth.

Sally, along with many others, believed that with all the effort put into exploring other planets, the same if not more effort should be put into understanding Earth and its continuous changes. She recommended studies that would help us be better prepared to protect our home planet and suggested that this could be done by putting more satellites in orbit to better study our planet.

Sally also made it quite clear in her space talks

around the country that she was strongly against weaponizing space—turning it into a place where one country could attack or harm another—and that doing so would be an eventual catastrophe for everyone. It would likely put our planet and lives in danger as well as harm safe space exploration.

Teaching

After finishing this one last project for NASA, Sally decided to go back into the academic world. She landed at the University of California San Diego, where she taught for many years, eventually becoming a physics professor and the director of the California Space Institute.

"I love the university environment . . . I love research, I love teaching," she said.

Despite all her amazing accomplishments, there were still people out there who didn't believe in Sally the professor. They didn't believe she could hack it as an educator. But as with everything else in her life, she persisted and proved them wrong. Many of her former students said that Sally had a way of teaching complicated matters that made them understandable—something her former high school teacher Dr. Mommaerts would have been proud of.

SALLY RIDE SCIENCE

One of Sally's greatest achievements was the project she started with her life partner as well as business partner, Tam O'Shaughnessy, a biologist. Sally and Tam were childhood friends who grew up playing tennis together. They kept in touch throughout the years and fell in love as adults. In

addition to tennis, they also shared a love of science. Sally would teach Tam about the stars and galaxies, and Tam would teach Sally about the land and animals. Together they decided to share their passion for science with kids. They both noticed the lack of fun books about science for young readers, so they decided to write some themselves. They thought: *Who better to write books like that than two scientists who love their work?*

Sally and Tam also noticed that as kids got

older their interest in science and math began to fade, especially for girls. The more they looked into it, the more they realized that society was pushing kids away from those subjects, telling them that it wasn't cool or fun to study science or math. So Sally, Tam and a couple of friends started their own company called Sally Ride Science to change that perception. Sally Ride Science was created to show young people (and even older ones!) that science is fascinating and innovative. They wrote more books and held events to connect kids with all types of science, in fun ways. Sally Ride Science continues that work today, and since its founding in 2001, it has reached millions of students and teachers.

....

Swinging on a Star

S ally Ride lived to be sixty-one years old.
She died at her home in La Jolla, California.
Sally had been diagnosed with pancreatic cancer
and battled it for seventeen months. She was sur-
vived by her partner of twenty-seven years, Tam
O'Shaughnessy, as well as her mother, her sister
and her sister's children.

Her ashes were buried next to her father's
grave in a cemetery in Santa Monica, California,

not too far from where she used to play tennis tournaments as a child. Bing Crosby's song "Swinging on a Star" played in the background as rose petals were placed on her grave.

Even after her death, Sally's legacies remain strong. Because of her initiatives, middle schoolers have had the chance to take pictures of Earth and then the moon from a camera that was on board first a space shuttle and then the International Space

Station. The projects were called EarthKam and MoonKam; today EarthKam has been renamed Sally Ride EarthKam in her memory and is still operating. Around 500,000 middle schoolers from more than seventy different countries have been able to participate. When the MoonKam was retired, it was sent crashing into the actual moon, and that area of the moon was then named Sally Ride Massif (which is another word for a kind of mountain). So the next time you look up at the moon, know that one section of that glorious celestial body is named after Sally.

Since Sally's time at NASA, there have been dozens of woman astronauts. Many of them thank Sally for giving them someone to look up to, someone who paved the way for them—someone who showed them that girls could do it too.

Sally taught kids that science can be cool, that not all scientists look like Albert Einstein or work alone in their basements or labs. Scientists explore, ask questions, devise experiments and discover new truths every day.

She once said, "We need to make science cool again." And Sally did just that.

Flying into space was not Sally's childhood dream, but it was a dream she found later and held close to her heart, and it was something that she worked hard for and cherished. As journalist and friend Lynn Sherr put it: "[Sally's] life reminds us that whatever our personal limits, there's something out there grander than we can measure, more marvelous than we can imagine; something just waiting to be explored." It's hard to imagine a more fitting tribute to Sally.

Sally Ride had many dreams in her life and she persisted in doing everything in her power to make those dreams come true. She had many challenges but she rose above them. Sally Ride persisted, and she would want you to do the same.

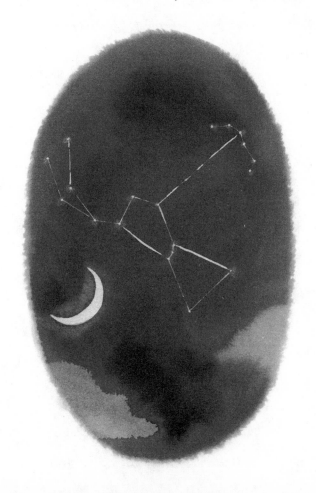

HOW YOU CAN PERSIST

by Atia Abawi

If you would like to honor Sally's memory or learn more about space and astronomy, there are many things you can do. Here are some:

1. Break gender barriers; inspire all your friends to reach for the stars.

2. If someone tries to say that someone can't do something, don't stay quiet. Tell them that anyone can do anything

as long as they keep persisting.

3. Don't stop learning new things. You never know what will become your passion. And while you explore new knowledge, visit sallyridescience .ucsd.edu and see what Sally was so passionate about.

4. Read one of the books that Sally wrote about space and science for young readers, and explore your curiosities.

5. Help the planet. We only have the one. Take care of it. Reuse and recycle. Be conscious of how you treat our planet's limited resources.

6. Look up at the stars and let your imagination race. And while you're

looking up, try to find Orion, Sally's
favorite constellation.

7. Dream big. Don't make the sky the
   limit; don't make the stars the limit.
   There are no limits to what you can do.

8. Tell your friends and family about Sally
   Ride, about her dreams, her passions
   and her persistence.

ACKNOWLEDGMENTS

I'm so grateful to be a part of the PerSisterhood team and have the honor to share the story of the trailblazer Sally Kristen Ride.

Chelsea Clinton, you created an incredible series and I am so excited to be a part of it. Gillian Flint and Alexandra Boiger, it is your beautiful art that brings Sally's story back to life.

I want to also extend my appreciation and love to my amazing "phamily" at Philomel and Penguin Random House. Jill Santopolo, thank you for always being my angel in publishing. Talia Benamy, Ellice Lee and Shanta Newlin, it is your hard work that gives us the ability to share these stories with the world. I also want to share my sincerest gratitude for the grueling work of the amazing copy editors and fact-checkers who helped in ensuring every bit of information we shared is correct and understandable to our readers: Shara Hardeson, Krista Ahlberg and Marinda Valenti.

Thank you, Tam O'Shaughnessy, for taking the time to speak to me about Sally. Thanks to your love and partnership with each other, you nurtured a new generation of scientists.

I'd also like to send my continued appreciation to my agent, Stephen Barbara, and the InkWell team for their consistent support, guidance and efforts.

And finally, to my life team: Conor, Arian and Elin—my dreams come true because of you and I thank God several times a day for the blessing of us. It is your support and love that keeps me persisting myself. Writing this book during the COVID-19 quarantine was not always easy, but it was something I cherished. It was one of the loudest, craziest, most beautiful times of my life. I know one day I'll write a book and I won't have the chorus of tiny voices screaming, "Mama! Mama! Mama!" in the background, but I'll close my eyes and think of this time and smile. I love you the mostest, I love you infinity forever.

∽ References ∽

BOOKS

O'Shaughnessy, Tam. *Sally Ride: A Photobiography of America's Pioneering Woman in Space*. New York: Roaring Brook, 2015.

Sherr, Lynn. *Sally Ride: America's First Woman in Space*. New York: Simon & Schuster, 2014.

INTERVIEW

O'Shaughnessy, Tam. Interview with the author.

August 2019.

WEBSITES

NPR. *Sally Ride, First American Woman
in Space, Is Dead.* July 23, 2012.
NPR. https://www.npr.org/sections
/thetwo-way/2012/07/23/157250870/sally-ride
-first-american-woman-in-space-is-dead?ps=cprs.

PBS NOVA. *An Interview with Sally Ride.* July
24, 2012. PBS. https://www.pbs.org/wgbh
/nova/video/an-interview-with-sally-ride.

ATIA ABAWI is a foreign news correspondent who spent ten years living and working in Afghanistan and then the Middle East. She was born to Afghan parents in West Germany and was raised in the United States. She is the critically acclaimed author of *The Secret Sky* and *A Land of Permanent Goodbyes*. She currently lives in California with her husband, Conor Powell, their son, Arian, and their daughter, Elin.

You can visit Atia Abawi online at
atiaabawi.com
and follow her on Twitter, Facebook and Instagram
@AtiaAbawi

GILLIAN FLINT has worked as a professional illustrator since earning an animation and illustration degree in 2003. Her work has since been published in the UK, USA and Australia. In her spare time, Gillian enjoys reading, spending time with her family and puttering about in the garden on sunny days. She lives in the northwest of England.

Courtesy of the illustrator

You can visit Gillian Flint online at
gillianflint.com
or follow her on Twitter
@GillianFlint
and on Instagram
@gillianflint_illustration

CHELSEA CLINTON is the author of the #1 *New York Times* bestseller *She Persisted: 13 American Women Who Changed the World*; *She Persisted Around the World: 13 Women Who Changed History*; *She Persisted in Sports: American Olympians Who Changed the Game*; *Don't Let Them Disappear: 12 Endangered Species Across the Globe*; *It's Your World: Get Informed, Get Inspired & Get Going!*; *Start Now!: You Can Make a Difference*; with Hillary Clinton, *Grandma's Gardens* and *Gutsy Women*; and, with Devi Sridhar, *Governing Global Health: Who Runs the World and Why?* She is also the Vice Chair of the Clinton Foundation, where she works on many initiatives, including those that help empower the next generation of leaders. She lives in New York City with her husband, Marc, their children and their dog, Soren.

You can follow Chelsea Clinton on Twitter
@ChelseaClinton
or on Facebook at
facebook.com/chelseaclinton

ALEXANDRA BOIGER has illustrated nearly twenty picture books, including the She Persisted books and *She Persisted Around the World*, both by Chelsea Clinton; the popular Tallulah series by Marilyn Singer; and the Max and Marla books, which she also wrote. Originally from Munich, Germany, she now lives outside of San Francisco, California, with her husband, Andrea, daughter, Vanessa, and two cats, Luiso and Winter.

You can visit Alexandra Boiger online at
alexandraboiger.com
on follow her on Instagram
@alexandra_boiger

Don't miss the rest of the books in the

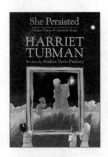

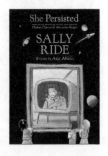
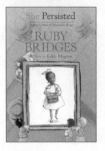

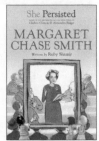

She Persisted series!

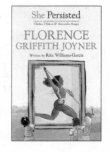

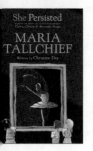

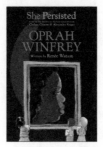